MAKING JEWELRY

Words by Eileen Deacon

Illustrations by Grahame Corbett

RAINTREE CHILDRENS BOOKS
Milwaukee • Toronto • Melbourne • London

Library of Congress Number: 77-7942

1 2 3 4 5 6 7 8 9 0 81 80 79 78 77

Printed and bound in the United States of America.

Library of Congress Cataloging in Publication Data

Deacon, Eileen.
    Making jewelry.

    Includes index.
    SUMMARY: Step-by-step instructions for making
original jewelry from available household objects.
        1.   Jewelry making — Juvenile literature.   [1.   Jewelry
making.   2.   Handicraft]   I.   Corbett, Grahame.
II.   Title.
TT212.D43   745.59'42   77-7942
ISBN 0-8393-0116-2 lib. bdg.

Contents

Necklaces

Here are some necklaces you could make. Thread them together with a needle and string or cord. Try thinking up your own ideas too.

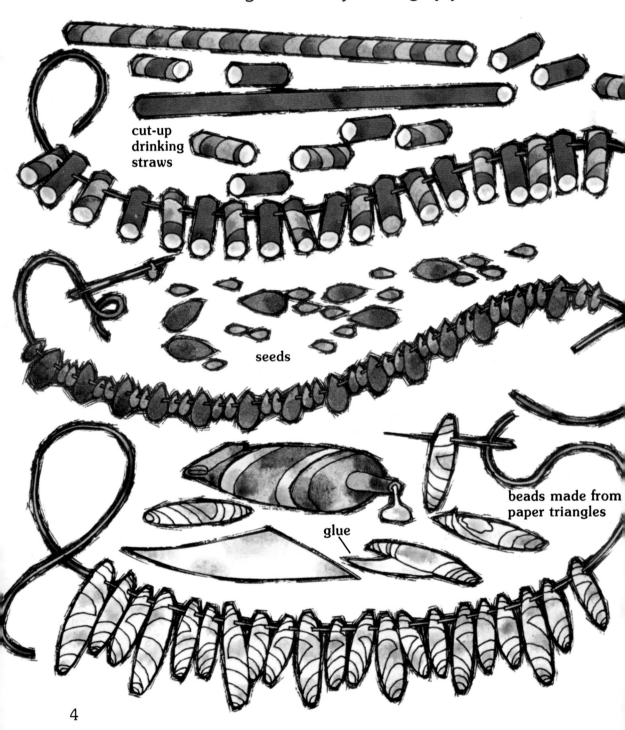

cut-up
drinking
straws

seeds

beads made from
paper triangles

glue

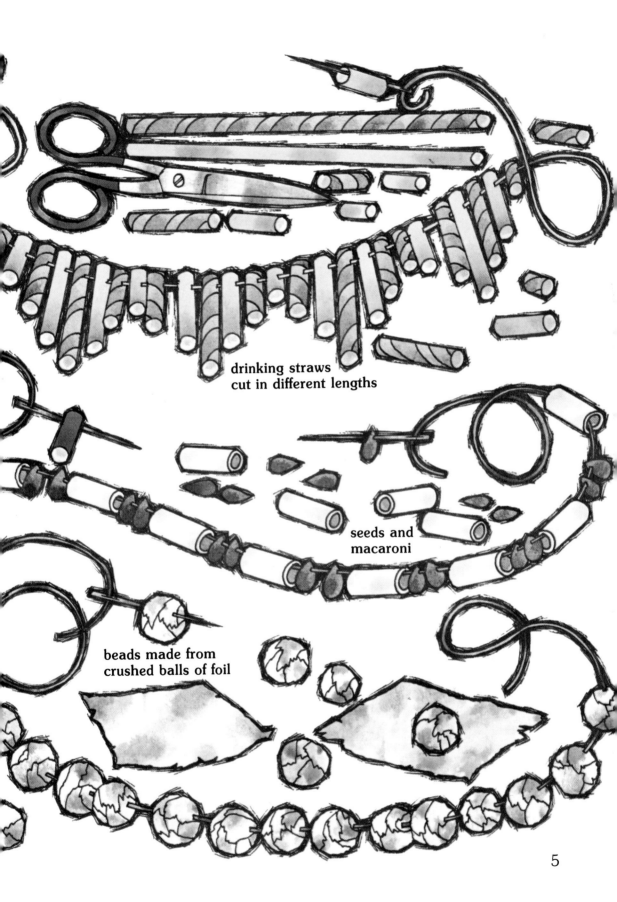

drinking straws
cut in different lengths

seeds and
macaroni

beads made from
crushed balls of foil

Pendants

Try making a pendant out of cardboard. The picture below shows what you will need. Cut the cardboard shapes out first. Then paint and decorate them. You could decorate your pendants with paper shapes, buttons, seeds, yarn or even pictures from magazines.

When the pendant is dry, cut some string or yarn to go around your neck. Glue the ends to the back of the cardboard.

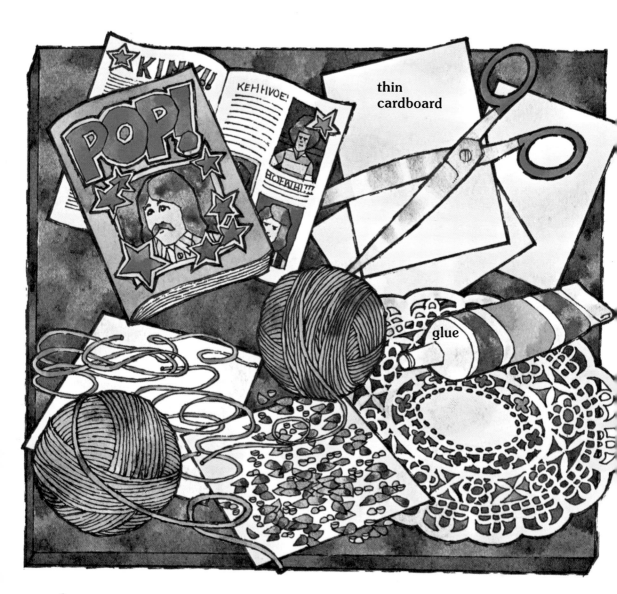

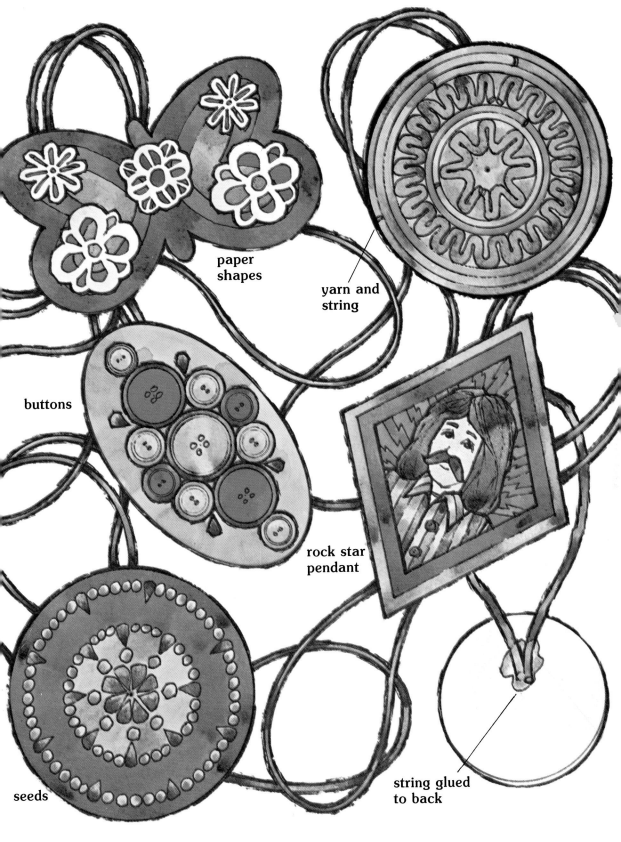

paper shapes

yarn and string

buttons

rock star pendant

seeds

string glued to back

7

Letter Pendants

You will need:

thin cardboard	brushes
scissors	glue (clear adhesive)
pencil	string to go around
paints	your neck

  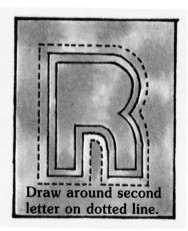

Draw around first letter on dotted line.

Draw around second letter on dotted line.

1 Cut out the first letter of your name from cardboard. Lay it on the cardboard again. Draw around it to make a bigger letter. Cut this out. Use it to make an even bigger letter.

2 Paint each letter.

3 Glue the letters together with the biggest one at the bottom.

ends of string
glued on

4 Glue the ends of the string to the back of the letters.
You could try making other shapes too.

Bracelets

You will need:

thin cardboard
pencil
ruler
scissors
glue (clear adhesive)
things to decorate
   your bracelets

1 Draw some strips on the cardboard. Cut the strips. If you want to cut patterns along the edges, it is easier to do this now.

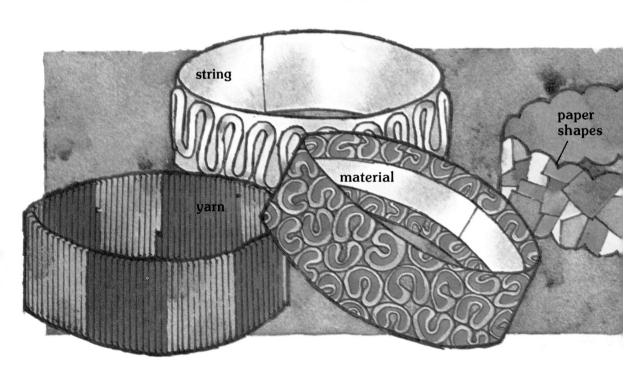

string

paper shapes

material

yarn

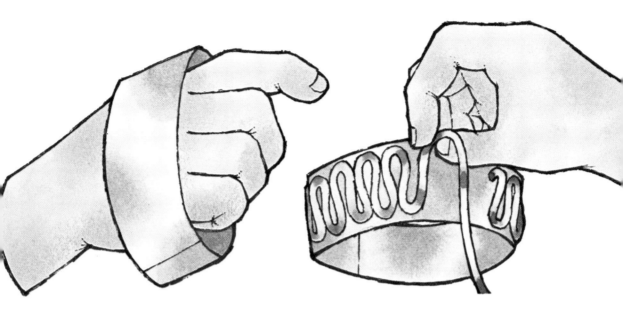

2 Glue the ends of the strips together to make bracelets. Make sure the bracelets will go over your wrist.

3 Paint and decorate your bracelets. The picture below may give you some ideas.

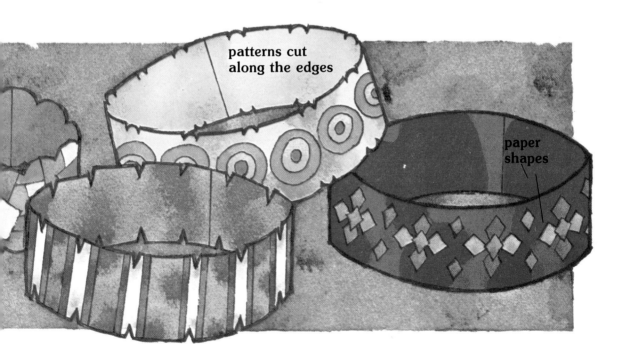

patterns cut along the edges

paper shapes

Gold and Silver Chains

Try making gold and silver chains from paper clips, safety pins or curtain rings. Think of other things to use too. Mix them in different ways. You could make pendants for the end of the chains.

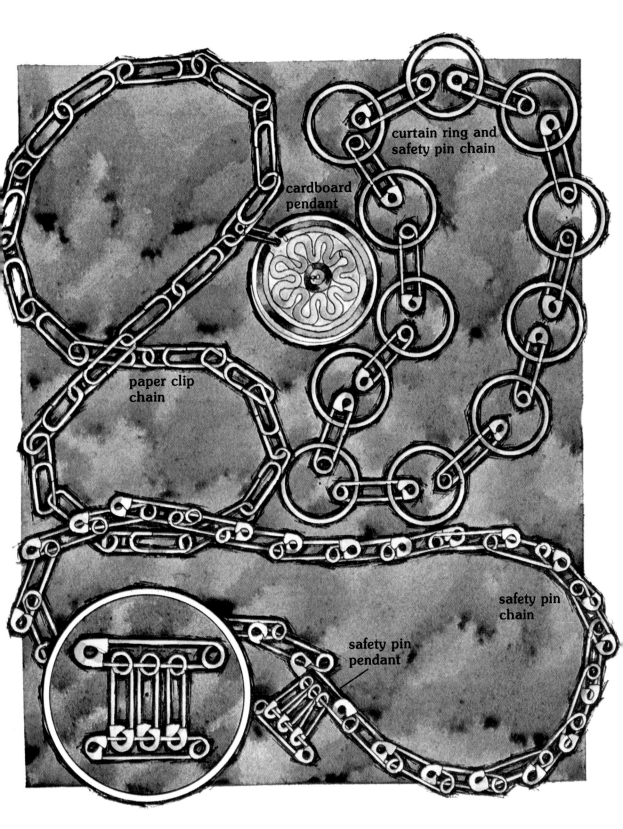

curtain ring and
safety pin chain

cardboard
pendant

paper clip
chain

safety pin
chain

safety pin
pendant

13

Curtain Ring Belt

Loop yarn over
front of rings
and out
around back.

Knot ends
together.

Look very carefully to see how this
belt is made. Make it from yarn
and curtain rings.

14

Rings

Here are some rings you can make from curtain rings. Wind yarn around the rings until they fit. Glue down the ends of the yarn. Glue things onto the front of your rings.

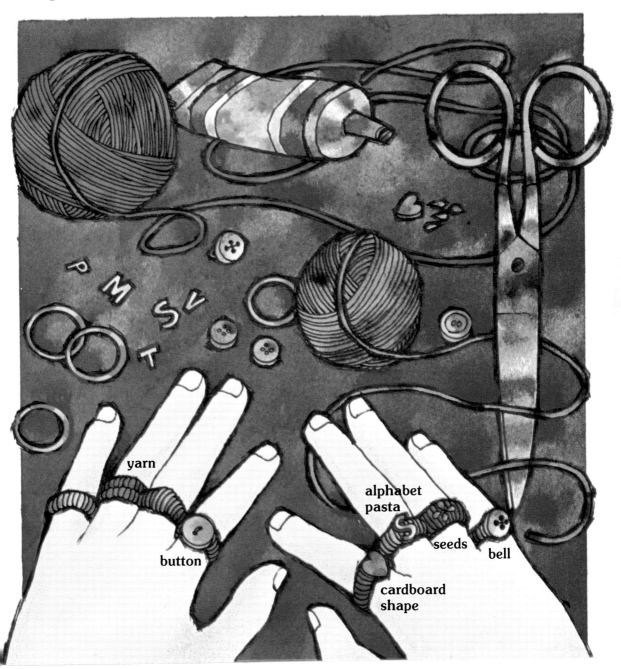

yarn

button

alphabet pasta

seeds

bell

cardboard shape

Pussy Cat Brooch

You will need:

yarn	material
scissors	big safety pin
big needle	glue (clear adhesive)

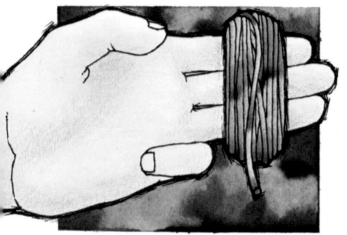

1 Wind yarn 100 times around three fingers.

2 Slip it off your fingers and tie it around the middle.

3 Cut the loops. Fluff the yarn out into a pom-pom.

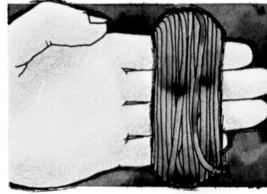

4 Make a bigger pom-pom. Wind yarn 125 times around four fingers.

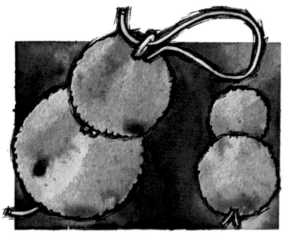

5 Sew the pom-poms together with yarn. Knot it underneath.

6 Tie on the safety pin.

7 Braid some yarn to make a tail. Sew it on.

8 Cut eyes, nose, mouth, and ears from material. Glue them on.

Pom-pom Jewelry

Make some pom-poms like the ones on the last two pages. Thread them together with yarn to make necklaces and bracelets.

Knot ends of yarn.

Hair Clips

Start a pom-pom like the ones opposite. Slip a bobby pin through the middle. Cut the loops. Fluff the yarn out.

Tie thread around clip.

Cut a shape from cardboard. Sew a bobby pin on the back. Now you can paint and decorate the front of the cardboard.

Braided Necklace

You will need:

six pieces of yarn
about 5 feet (1.52 meters)
long
some extra yarn
four small bells
scissors

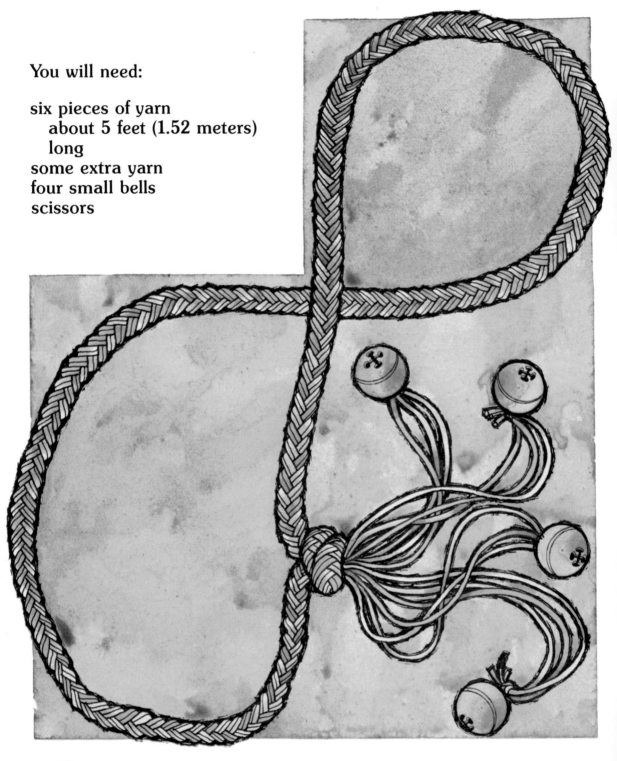

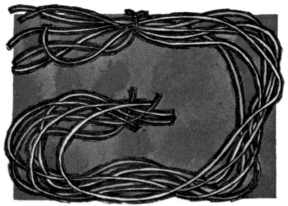

1 Tie the six pieces of yarn together at one end.

2 Divide the wool evenly into three and braid. Tie end of the braid.

3 Tie the braid into a loop.

4 Divide the ends evenly into four.

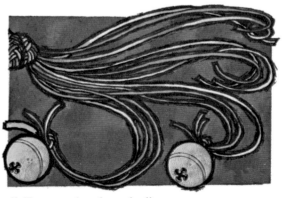

5 Tie on the four bells.

6 Trim the ends of the yarn.

Arab Belt

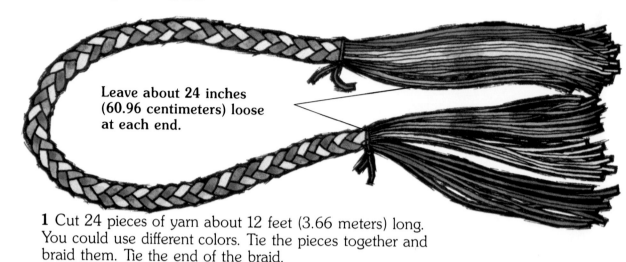

Leave about 24 inches
(60.96 centimeters) loose
at each end.

1 Cut 24 pieces of yarn about 12 feet (3.66 meters) long.
You could use different colors. Tie the pieces together and
braid them. Tie the end of the braid.

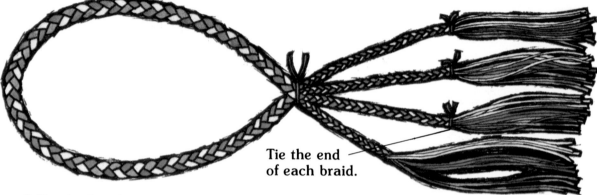

Tie the end
of each braid.

2 Tie the braid into a loop. Divide the ends evenly into four and
make four braids. There should be 12 ends in each braid.

3 Divide the ends of the braids into four again and braid them.
There should be three ends in each braid.

4 Tie pieces of yarn around the bottom of the loop and the bottom of the first four braids. Wind the yarn around, covering any loose ends.

5 Using a needle, thread in the ends of the yarn. Trim off any loose ends.

6 Now put the belt around your waist. Slot the braids through the loop as in the picture. Let the braids hang down in front.

Peel Jewelry

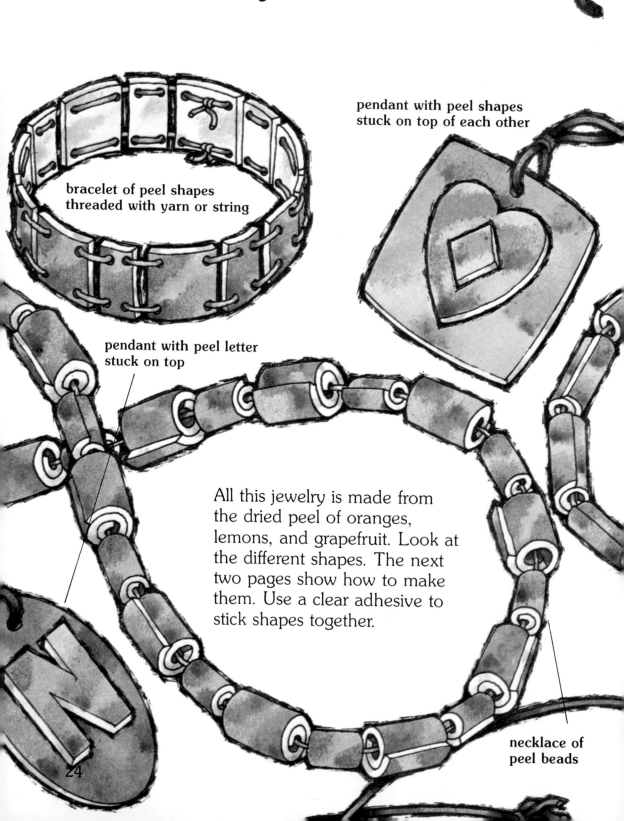

bracelet of peel shapes threaded with yarn or string

pendant with peel shapes stuck on top of each other

pendant with peel letter stuck on top

All this jewelry is made from the dried peel of oranges, lemons, and grapefruit. Look at the different shapes. The next two pages show how to make them. Use a clear adhesive to stick shapes together.

necklace of peel beads

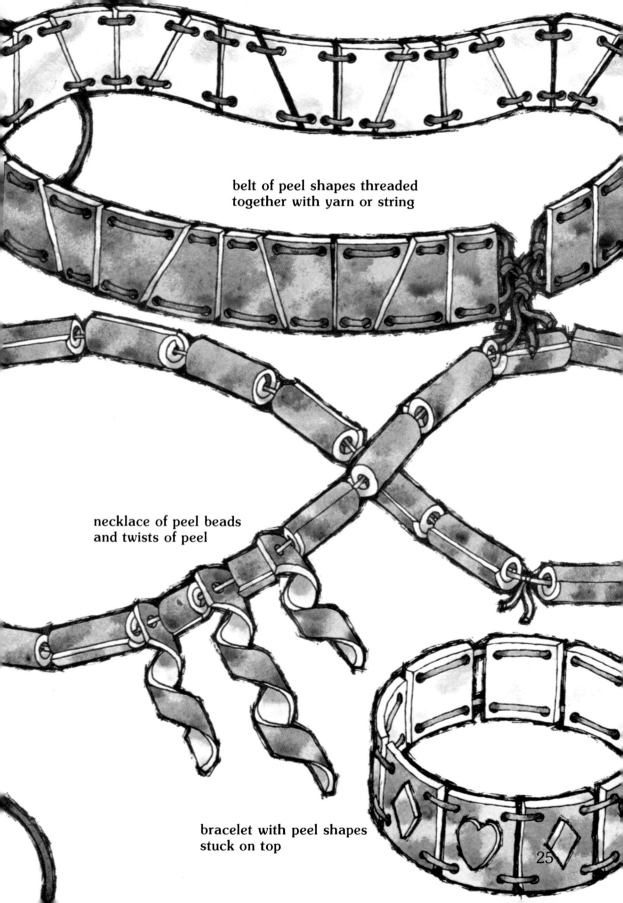

belt of peel shapes threaded
together with yarn or string

necklace of peel beads
and twists of peel

bracelet with peel shapes
stuck on top

Drying Peel

You will need:

oranges, lemons
or grapefruit
knife
knitting needles

sticky tape
sheets of newspaper
some heavy books

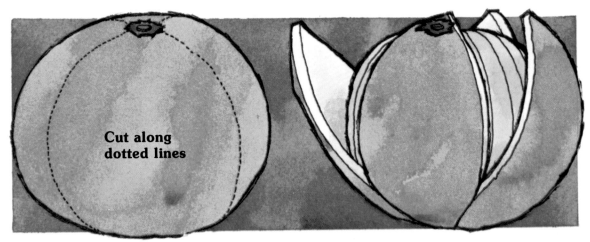

Cut along dotted lines

1 Cut the peel of each fruit into four.

2 Cut out shapes from some of the peel. Make holes in some
of the shapes with a knitting needle.

3 Cut the rest of the peel into strips. If the peel is very thick, ask a grown-up to help cut some off the back. Wind the strips around the needles. Tape the strips down.

4 Let all the pieces dry in a warm place. Put the flat pieces between the sheets of newspaper. Put heavy books on top.

5 Now you can make the dry peel shapes into all kinds of jewelry. If you want some ideas, turn back to the last two pages.

Papier Mâché Brooch

You will need:

teaspoon of
   wallpaper paste
cup of water
cardboard
scissors
big safety pin

glue (clear adhesive)
thin paper or newspaper
stiff brush
thin string
paints
paintbrushes

1 Mix the paste and the water.
Leave for 15 minutes.

2 Cut a shape from the cardboard.
Cut a small square too.

3 Glue the square over the pin on
the back of the cardboard.

4 Cut strips from the paper.
Paint paste on both sides with
the stiff brush.

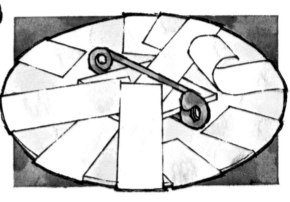

5 Lay the strips all over the cardboard. Smooth down each layer.

6 Lay strips all over the back too. Let all the strips dry.

7 Dip a long piece of string in the paste.

8 Arrange it in a pattern on the brooch. Let the brooch dry.

9 Paint your brooch. Here are some different patterns and colors you could try.

Papier Mâché Beads

You will need:

teaspoon of
   wallpaper paste
cup of water
thin paper or newspaper
scissors
ruler
stiff brush for painting on
   paste
greased knitting needles
paints
brushes
strong thread
big needle

1 Mix the paste with the water. Leave for 15 minutes.

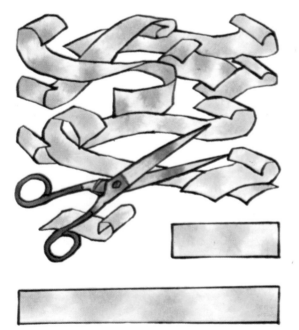

2 Cut the paper into strips of two different lengths.

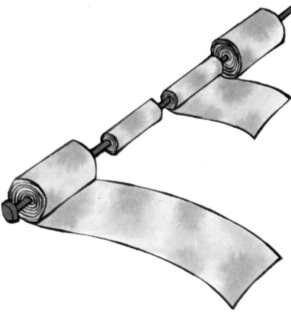

3 Paint paste on both sides. Wind around the needles. Leave to dry.

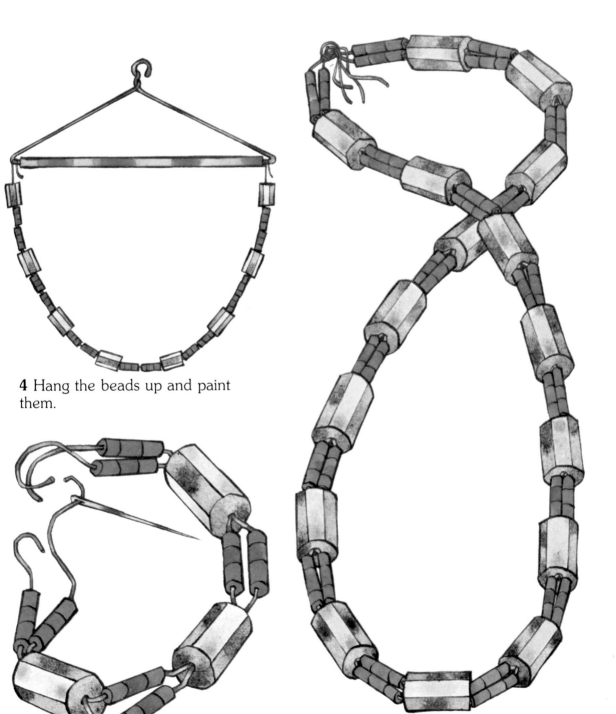

4 Hang the beads up and paint them.

5 When they are dry, thread them together with the needle.

6 You could make bracelets or a necklace like this one. Think of other ways to thread the beads.

31

Enameling

You will need:

one egg white
3 ounces (85 grams)
   icing sugar
bowl
egg beater
paper cups

spoon
varnish
soft paintbrush
any flat jewelry
   you want to decorate
poster paints

1 Beat the egg white until it is quite stiff.

2 Add the sugar.

3 Beat the mixture again. Put some into each paper cup.

4 Add a little paint. Add a different color to each pot.

5 Dribble some colors onto each piece of jewelry.

6 Leave the pieces to dry overnight.

7 Varnish the pieces when the enamel is hard.

Egyptian Collar

This man lived in Egypt long ago. He is wearing a collar covered with gold and jewels. If you want to make your own Egyptian collar, look at the next three pages.

1 You will need all these things: big piece of material, tape measure, string, two pens, scissors, glue, two safety pins.

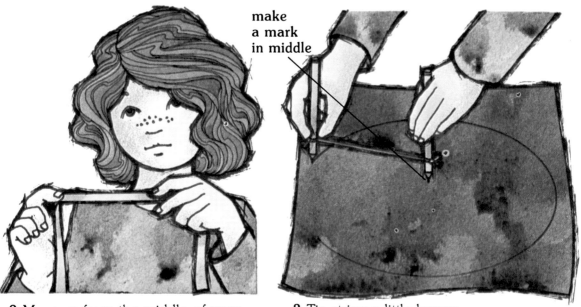

make
a mark
in middle

2 Measure from the middle of your neck to the end of your shoulder.

3 Tie string a little longer than measurement between pens. Draw a circle on the cloth.

4 Measure around your neck. Divide measurement by four, into quarters.

mark in the middle

5 Tie string just over one quarter long between pens. Draw a circle in middle of the first one.

6 Cut the collar out. Cut a slit in the collar so it will go around your neck.

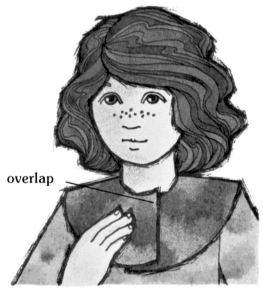

overlap

7 Try it on for size. Leave an overlap of about 2 inches (5.08 centimeters).

8 Now glue on some decorations. You could use yarn, string, buttons or curtain rings.

9 Fasten the collar on with the safety pins. Turn the pins around to the back.

Jewelry Box

1 You will need all these things: shoe box and lid, scissors, two Band-Aids, glue, paper fastener, tin foil, string.

2 Cut the sides off the lid. Fasten the lid on the box with the Band-Aids.

3 Make a hole in the lid. Tie string through it in a loop.

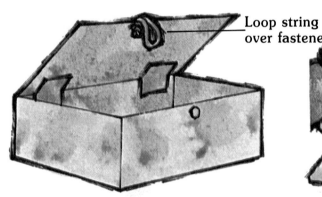

Loop string over fastener.

4 Push the paper fastener through the front of the box. Fold the ends back inside.

5 Glue pieces of foil all over the box. You could glue on other decorations too.

Things to Remember

Before you start
If you are going to use paint or glue, cover your work space with newspaper or a plastic tablecloth. Wear an apron or an old shirt. It would also help to have a cloth or tissues to wipe your hands.

When you finish
Clean everything up. Wipe up any paint marks. Throw away the things you do not want. Keep the things you think might be useful later.

Gluing
The best glue to use on all the projects in this book is a clear adhesive, such as Elmer's Glue-All.

Painting
Any paint you can mix with water will work on paper, cardboard and soft things, such as yarn and string. (Make the paint quite thick for yarn and string.) For hard, shiny things, such as plastic, the best paint is acrylic paint. You could also use up old gloss paint or enamel paint. Always put the tops and

lids back on paint jars and tubes. Then the paint will not get hard.

Varnishing
If you have used poster, powder or emulsion paint, varnishing it will make it last longer. Model-makers' varnish is quite cheap. You could buy it in a hobby shop or dime store.

Remember to keep the top on the bottle of varnish. Otherwise it will become too thick to use.

Cleaning brushes

Always clean your brushes after using them. Rinse them out in cold water if you have used poster or powder paint, or acrylic or emulsion paint. Rinse them out in turpentine if you have used gloss paint, enamel paint or varnish.

To keep your brushes really clean and soft, wash them with soap and cold water after rinsing them.

Making more jewelry

Try thinking up your own ideas for jewelry. Look at things around you and see if they give you any ideas. Look at things that are going to be thrown away. Save the ones you like and think might be useful.

Look at the things in the picture opposite. What kinds of jewelry could you make with them?

Make a collection of the things you would like to use. Keep your collection in a big box. You will soon have enough things to make some jewelry.

tops

screws

corks

stones

pins

washers

twigs

nails

thumbtacks

string

Strange Jewelry

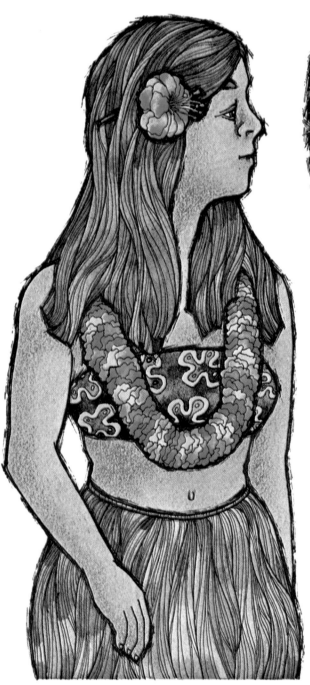

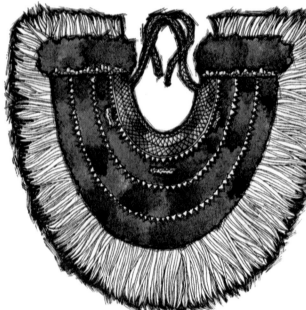

This necklace is made of feathers. It comes from Tahiti. It was once worn in battle.

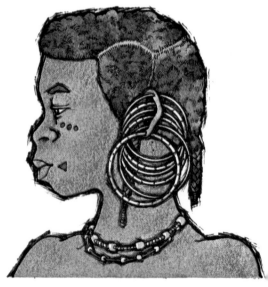

This girl is wearing a necklace made from flowers. It is called a *lei*.

Holes have been pierced down the side of this woman's ears. She wears a ring through each hole.

This Indian girl is wearing a
ring through the side of her nose.
She also has rings on her toes.

Here is an Apache Indian. He is
doing a dance. He wears bells on
his legs.

This girl is wearing hoops of grass covered with beads. This shows that she is old enough to get married.

apron

This girl has just been married. She wears a special cloak and apron, both covered with beads.

44

pendant

collar

Here is some jewelry made from
shells. Pendants like this were
made from clam shells and collars
like this from conch shells.

This man comes from South
America. He wears a piece of
wood in his lower lip. It is
called a *labret*.

This woman is a Padaung.
Padaung means "long neck."
Padaung women wear metal rings
around their necks. The rings stretch
their necks and make them longer.
They also wear rings on their legs.

Lucky Jewels

There have been many strange stories and beliefs about jewels. People once believed that jewels had all kinds of magic powers. They also thought there was a lucky jewel or "birthstone" for each month. To find out about your birthstone, look for the month when you were born.

January: garnet
Some garnets were supposed to shine in the dark.

February: amethyst
An amethyst would make the wearer a good person.

March: bloodstone
A bloodstone would make the wearer wise.

April: diamond
A diamond would protect the wearer from evil, especially if worn on the left side.

May: emerald
Emeralds were supposed to improve the eyesight.

June: pearl
Some people once thought pearls were the tears of angels which had fallen into the sea.

July: ruby
Some people believed that a ruby placed in cold water would make the water boil.

August: sardonyx
The sardonyx was supposed to protect the wearer from magic.

September: sapphire
The owner of a sapphire could not be taken prisoner.

October: opal
An opal would make the wearer invisible to his or her enemies.

November: topaz
Some people believed that a topaz placed in boiling water would make the water cold.

December: turquoise
A turquoise would protect the wearer from injury in a fall.

garnet   amethyst   bloodstone   diamond   emerald   pearl

ruby   sardonyx   sapphire   opal   topaz   turquoise

Index